C is for ...

Cardinal

Adventure Publications
Cambridge, Minnesota

Dedication

To the children of the world who love nature as much as I do.

All photos by Stan Tekiela

Edited by Ryan Jacobson
Cover and book design by Jonathan Norberg

10 9 8 7 6 5

C is for Cardinal
Copyright © 2016 by Stan Tekiela
Published by Adventure Publications
An imprint of AdventureKEEN
310 Garfield Street South
Cambridge, Minnesota 55008
(800) 678-7006
www.adventurepublications.net
Printed in China
ISBN 978-1-59193-533-9 (pbk.)

C is for ...

Cardinal

If a robin sees itself in a window, it will sometimes fight its own reflection.

A robin's eyes are on the sides of its head. To look forward, it turns its head sideways.

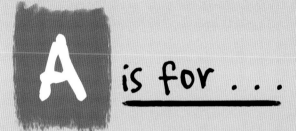

A is for . . .

American Robin

B is for ...

Bluebird

You can feed bluebirds
with a small tray
of mealworms.

Many bird lovers build nest
boxes. Bluebirds like to live
in these wooden homes.

Young cardinals have gray bills. The mommy and daddy have red bills.

C

is for . . .

Cardinal

A cardinal looks like it
wears a black mask.

Downies drum on hollow branches to tell other woodpeckers to stay away.

A woodpecker's tongue is very long. It gets bugs out of cracks in trees.

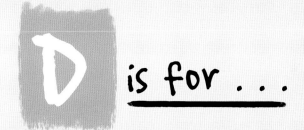

D is for . . .

Downy
Woodpecker

E is for . . .

Eagle

Eagles make their nests bigger each year. Their nests can weigh as much as a polar bear!

Eagle claws are called talons. They are strong enough to pull a fish out of the water!

A flicker is a kind
of woodpecker.

Flickers eat ants and
beetles off the ground.
Other woodpeckers find
their food in trees.

F is for . . .

Flicker

G is for . . .

Goldfinch

Goldfinches love a special food called thistle seed.

Goldfinches live in groups. If you see one, you'll probably see a bunch of them!

Hummingbirds flap their wings so fast that they sound like bees.

Hummingbirds can fly backward! No other bird can.

H is for . . .

Hummingbird

I is for . . .

Indigo
Bunting

Indigo Bunting boys are not actually blue. The feathers look blue because of how light reflects off the feathers.

Only the daddy looks blue. The mommy is brown.

Jays can make sounds like a hawk. This scares away other birds.

Blue Jays are very smart.

J is for . . .

Jay

If you see a Killdeer that looks hurt, it might be tricking you. Killdeer do this to lead animals away from their nests.

K is for . . .

Killdeer

As soon as the babies hatch, they start to follow the mommy and daddy around to find food.

L is for . . .

Loon

Baby loons learn to swim right after hatching. They rest on a parent's back when they get tired.

Loons can't walk very well, but they are great swimmers!

A meadowlark's song sounds like a flute.

Meadowlarks have a pretty black spot on their yellow chests. It looks like a bib.

M is for . . .

Meadowlark

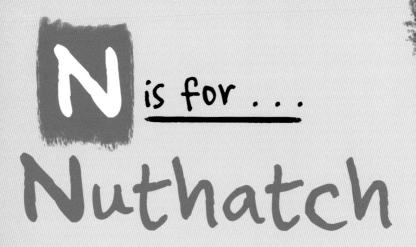

N is for ...

Nuthatch

The nuthatch has an extra-long toe that points backward. It helps the bird climb headfirst down a tree.

Being upside down helps nuthatches find bugs to eat that other birds can't see.

Orioles weave a nest
that's shaped like a
sock or sleeping bag.
It's a warm, safe and
comfortable place
to grow up.

Bird watchers love orioles.
They feed the birds grape jelly
and oranges cut in half.

O is for . . .

Oriole

P is for . . .

Purple Martin

Purple Martins are swift hunters. They can catch bugs in midair.

Purple Martins usually live in nest boxes that people make for them.

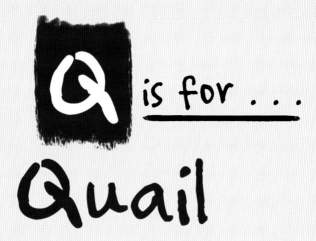

Q is for ...

Quail

Quails can sleep with one eye open. This lets them watch for danger.

A boy quail has a white throat. A girl has a tan throat.

Rose-breasted Grosbeaks are named for the red spot on the males' chests.

A grosbeak's huge bill cracks open seeds to eat.

R is for . . .

Rose-breasted
Grosbeak

S is for . . .

Scarlet Tanager

Boy Scarlet Tanagers are red for only part of the year. They turn yellow in the Fall.

There are many kinds of tanagers in the world. Most live in places that are very hot and sunny.

Trumpeter Swans are very big birds. They have more feathers than any other bird in the country.

A Trumpeter Swan's call sounds like a trumpet.

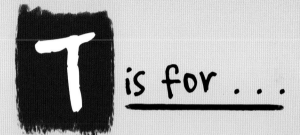

T is for . . .

Trumpeter
Swan

U is for . . .

Upland Sandpiper

Upland Sandpipers are shorebirds that don't live at the shore.

Sandpipers like to look for food in prairie land after a fire.

The vulture has no feathers on its head. This helps it stay clean while eating.

A vulture's wingspan is longer than most people are tall.

V is for . . .

Vulture

 is for . . .

Wild Turkey

Wild Turkeys
see much
better than
people do.

A crossbill has a bill shaped like an X. It helps the bird open pinecones, so it can eat the seeds inside.

Crossbills sometimes hang upside down to reach pinecones.

X is for . . .

X-shaped
Beak

Y is for . . .

Yellowthroat

In spring, the boys do a crazy dance. They jump in and out of tall grass to show off for the girls!

The yellowthroat is a kind of warbler.

Greater Sage-Grouse

Purple Gallinule

There are lots of zany-looking birds in nature. These are just four of the many kinds!

Wood Duck

Roseate Spoonbill

Z is for . . .

Zany-looking

Below are some notes on the colorful and interesting selection of birds presented in this book.

American Robin The American Robin is the state bird of three states. It is one of the most common birds in the U.S. and Canada.

Eastern Bluebird The Eastern Bluebird, the Western Bluebird and the Mountain Bluebird are in the U.S. and Canada. The Eastern and Western Bluebirds are blue with red chests. The Mountain Bluebird is all blue.

Northern Cardinal The Northern Cardinal is the state bird of seven states. It is one of only two kinds of cardinals in the U.S. The other is the Pyrrhuloxia, which lives in the deserts of the Southwest.

Downy Woodpecker The Downy Woodpecker looks a lot like the Hairy Woodpecker, but the Downy Woodpecker is smaller and has a shorter bill.

Bald Eagle There are two types of eagles in the U.S. and Canada: the Bald Eagle and the Golden Eagle. The Bald Eagle has a white head. The Golden Eagle's head is brown, like its body.

Northern Flicker The Northern Flicker is one of two kinds of flickers in the U.S. The other is known as a Gilded Flicker. The Northern Flicker says, "Wacka-wacka."

American Goldfinch The American Goldfinch is the most common kind of goldfinch. The Lesser Goldfinch and the Lawrence's Goldfinch are only found in parts of the southwestern U.S.

Ruby-throated Hummingbird There are 16 different kinds of hummingbirds in the U.S. and Canada. The Ruby-throated Hummingbird is one of the most common. It lives east of the Rocky Mountains.

Indigo Bunting Male Indigo Buntings look blue during spring and summer, but they change colors in the fall. They become light brown, much like the color of female Indigo Buntings.

Blue Jay Jays are related to crows and are considered some of the smartest birds in the U.S. and Canada. The Blue Jay can sound like a hawk to scare away other birds.

Killdeer A Killdeer is a trickster. It pretends to be hurt by faking that it has a broken wing. When other animals get close to it, the Killdeer flies away.

Common Loon The Common Loon, the Arctic Loon, the Pacific Loon, the Red-throated Loon and the Yellow-billed Loon live in the U.S. and Canada. The Common Loon is the most common kind of loon to see.

Eastern Meadowlark The Eastern Meadowlark and the Western Meadowlark almost look the same. Many people think the best way to tell them apart is by their songs.

White-breasted Nuthatch The White-breasted Nuthatch is one of four kinds in the U.S. The others are the Brown-headed Nuthatch, the Pygmy Nuthatch and the Red-breasted Nuthatch.

Baltimore Oriole There are nine kinds of orioles. All of them look very much alike, except their orange coloring is slightly different. Baltimore Orioles sing beautiful songs.

Purple Martin Male Purple Martins look glossy purple, but female Purple Martins aren't purple at all. They are brown and gray in color.

Bobwhite Quail In some states, people call this bird the Bobwhite Quail. Its common name isn't "quail" at all. It's actually the Northern Bobwhite.

Rose-breasted Grosbeak The name "grosbeak" refers to this bird's large bill. It's perfect for crushing seeds to eat. Grosbeaks also eat insects and fruit.

Scarlet Tanager This bright red bird is hard to confuse with any other bird. It is smaller than a cardinal and has black wings. The females are not red, though. They are yellow.

Trumpeter Swan The Trumpeter Swan is the largest waterbird in the U.S. and Canada. It looks a lot like the Tundra Swan and the Mute Swan. It can be hard to tell them apart.

Upland Sandpiper The Upland Sandpiper lives in grasslands, not on the shores, like other sandpipers. The Upland Sandpiper used to be called the Upland Plover.

Turkey Vulture There are two kinds of vultures in the U.S. The adult Turkey Vulture has a red head, and the adult Black Vulture has a black head.

Wild Turkey The Wild Turkey can fly very fast, almost as fast as a car on the highway. It can also take off from a standing position, without a running start.

Red Crossbill Crossbills are named for the way the upper and lower parts of their beaks cross. There are two types of crossbills in the U.S. and Canada: the Red Crossbill and the White-winged Crossbill.

Common Yellowthroat It is hard to confuse this bird with any other. It has a black "mask" and a bright yellow chest. Its song sounds like "witchity-witchity-witchity-witchity."

Purple Gallinule This bird looks zany because of its bright blue and purple colors. Plus, it has long legs and long toes.

Greater Sage-Grouse When displaying for females, the male Greater Sage-Grouse fans his tail, droops his wings and inflates his chest. He looks like he is wearing a fur collar.

Wood Duck The male Wood Duck is one of the most handsome of all ducks because of his patchwork of colors.

Roseate Spoonbill The Roseate Spoonbill is pink in color, but it is not related to the flamingo, as many people believe.

About the Author

Naturalist, wildlife photographer and writer Stan Tekiela is the originator of the popular Wildlife and Nature Appreciation book series that includes *Wild Birds*. Stan has authored more than 190 educational books, including field guides, quick guides, nature books, children's books, playing cards and more, presenting many species of animals and plants.

With a Bachelor of Science degree in Natural History from the University of Minnesota and as an active professional naturalist for more than 30 years, Stan studies and photographs wildlife throughout the United States and Canada. He has received various national and regional awards for his books and photographs. Also a well-known columnist and radio personality, his syndicated column appears in more than 25 newspapers, and his wildlife programs are broadcast on a number of Midwest radio stations. Stan can be followed on Facebook and Twitter. He can be contacted via www.naturesmart.com.